MW01594885

Made For More

Made For More

Removing the Limitations That Keep You From Being Your Best

Gary Rogers

This book is dedicated to My Paula.
After 50 years of marriage, she is my best friend and mutual follower of Jesus. The content of this book began as a personal study and so intrigued me, it became a frequent topic of conversation. Paula encouraged and then insisted the writing of this book. It would not have happened without her.

Leah's Story

Forward

Competition thrives in our culture. When you're standing against a fence and waiting to hear the team captain call out the first name, only one can be the first choice. That leaves everyone else on common ground. How should you respond to not being the first choice or not being number one? What do you do when you have no encouragement around you? Where do you find strength to learn from failure and strive to be better?

Pick a topic from professional athlete to entertainer, from successful business owner to elected politician; and you'll find that more tried and didn't make it than those who tried and succeeded. Most of us would call it childish to respond with, "If I'm not number one, then I quit!" Or, "If I don't make it the first try, then I'm giving up!"

What do you do when you discover you don't have all the gifts, talents, and abilities of those around you? How do you respond when you are labeled as lacking? What do you do when there is no encouragement nor support from those closest in your life? How do you respond when being number one is not an option? What do you do when you fail at you first attempt? Do you give up? Do you quit? Or do you allow yourself to be convinced that you were **Made For More**?

Abraham is recognized in Christianity as the father of faith. He received from God a covenant promise that through him all the world would be blessed. (**Genesis 12:1-4**) This world-wide blessing for all nations and all people would be fulfilled in the life and death and resurrection of one of his descendants, Jesus.

Abraham and Sarah had a son named Isaac, and he was to carry the covenant promise. (**Genesis 17:19**) Isaac married Rebekah and had twin boys Esau and Jacob. Jacob was God's choice to carry the promise, but the competition between the twin brothers

2

escalated to a murder threat, and the family sent Jacob to live with his uncle Laban far from home. Laban had two daughters. The older was named Leah, and the younger was Rachel.

Leah began with no advantages in life. She was not the prettiest. She was not her father's favorite. Her home life was so sad, her father used her as compensation for a business contract. After her first night of marriage, her husband let her and everyone else know how disappointed he was in her as his wife. Her husband felt cheated, because he was tricked into marrying her.

Leah teaches us how to thrive when not the first choice. She was definitely not number one. Leah teaches us how to get up from rejection and failure and try again. She overcame desperation, even though she went along with the plan to deceive her future husband. She overcame the heartbreak in knowing her husband loved her sister most. She overcame an inferior identity from being compared to a beautiful sister and coming out lacking. Leah ultimately found her purpose and joy in life, and in the end received all she had hoped for.

Leah's thriving as a second string wife not only shaped her life with fulfillment and tremendous accomplishments, but influences all our lives today. If Leah had not gained her victory our world would be much different. Few people have had as much impact on our world as this lady rarely mentioned in the Bible.

In the study of Leah, I have found parallels to my personal life. From being raised in a dysfunctional and abusive home, to searching for my personal identity and purpose, Leah and I have much in common. You may find that you do also.

Leah's struggles and victories have helped me to understand God's plan in guiding me through both good and bad. I believe an examination of her life can be relevant for you. Through her story you will see how God's purpose for her life became clear. In realizing that purpose, she received both fulfillment and joy. From a young woman with low self-esteem to her later years of enjoying her greatest desire, you will see the difficulties and tragedies, accomplishments and victories that shaped her life.

Let me invite you to join me in this study of an amazing lady named Leah who knew in spite of what others thought or said about her, she was *Made For More*.

1. Starting Point

Leah was like many of us who have wondered why God put us on this earth. She had every right to ask: "Does God love me?" "Is God a good God?" "Why has God treated me like this?"

Her name came from a Hebrew word meaning weary, tired, or faint. Even her name labeled her as having low energy, minimal drive, and little to no ambition. Her starting point was low and had little expectation of improving.

Genesis 29:17 – *"Leah had weak eyes, but Rachel was lovely in form, and beautiful."* NIV

It is hard to read this verse without seeing a comparison. Rachel was described as a stand out in her appearance, Leah was not. Rachel looked in a mirror and saw an attractive woman with a beautiful body that gained admiring attention. Leah looking in a mirror saw no natural beauty. She saw nothing to gain the attention and love of a man. She saw

7

a young woman "without" in comparison to a sister "with."

Most of us can relate more with Leah than Rachel. When you look around in comparison, someone else has more God-given talent and abilities. Someone else is more qualified and more suitable. Someone else has a better education and credentials. Someone else has been given greater opportunities and has a greater potential for success. Someone else captures attention in the evaluation while you seem to blend in with the crowd.

Few make valedictorian. There is only one quarterback. Not many are given a full ride academic or athletic scholarship. Of those stand-out college athletes few are even considered by a professional sports team. CEO is a position reserved for the one who made it to the top of the company. Hero is a label only given when you happen to be at the right place at the right time, and you're prepared to do the right thing in the right circumstance.

You must recognize you were not born with the natural ability to be number one. You must conclude that not everything in life will come easy. You must admit the competition is great and you are lacking. Now will you declare defeat without even competing? Will you give up without a fight? Will you whine, moan, and groan listing every excuse why you should not show up?

Character is revealed when you are willing to see the truth and deal with it. Recognizing and accepting truth should not take you into depression, discouragement, and defeat. So what if you have little natural ability? That just means you'll have to work harder. So what if the competition is great? That just means when you win you will be better than great. Truth is the foundation you build upon. Truth is the starting place that change comes from.

Faith is starting at a place where failure looks inevitable.

Moses leading some 3 million people across the desert looked like failure. Joshua leading an inexperienced army against the fortified city of Jericho looked like a failure. David preparing to fight a giant looked like failure. Peter responding to Jesus' invitation to walk on water looked like failure. Over and over faith starts from a place of potential failure.

Leah's life started from a place where failure looked inevitable, but she convinced herself that she was **Made For More**.

******

I was born the youngest of three children in a home of an abusive father. My dad was an angry man filled with a hate that I would not know the origins of until he shared the details with me from his death bed.

Jesus became my Lord and Savior at Vacation Bible School when I was seven years old. That time of conversion was very real to me. At seven years old I became a Christian and really meant it. I have been a believer ever since. I've made many mistakes and seen more than one failure, but Jesus has been Lord of my life since that day.

My father wanted nothing to do with God. He permitted my mother and us three kids to go to church, but he made it very clear to not expect him to attend, and don't ask. My brother was two years older and at fifteen he decided to stop attending church. My sister was already married and out of the house, so at thirteen it was my mother and me going to church alone.

My older brother and dad began to form a tight bond with fishing, cars, and Sunday work projects. It quickly became "men don't go to church". At this time my father became even more angry and abusive, but now I was the only target.

There were repeated beatings, consistent cussing out, and even my plate at the table was thrown into my lap. After a few years, I was forced to make a decision. Would I give up my Christian witness, and let my personal anger bring retaliation in fighting back? Would I abandon my Christian stand and join him and my brother to seek his approval? Or would I stand firm in my love commitment to Jesus and keep taking his abuse?

The decision I made was to quit seeking the approval of someone who would never give it. Dad would never give me approval for being a Christian. If I wanted his approval I would have to share his anger and hatred for the church and everything that represented God. That was an approval I didn't want. I chose to not care what he thought. I chose to stand as a Christian and take his abuse. I chose to try with all that was in me to represent Jesus to a hard, hateful, angry man.

Quit seeking the approval of someone who would never give it.

You may be like me and can identify with a young lady name Leah who had little to work with from the life she was given. But like Leah, I believed I was *Made For More*.

2. Search For Value

When Jacob reached the age that was time to look for a wife, his parents wanted him to marry from their people and not the people of the land where they had relocated. So Jacob traveled back to the place of their heritage. There God directed him to the house of his uncle, Laban.

Leah was Laban's oldest daughter. Laban was a businessman driven by financial success. When Jacob showed up, Laban saw dollar signs. He saw a young, healthy man he could use for financial gain. After working without wages for a month, Laban was ready to secure a long-term arrangement that would keep Jacob on his payroll. He asked Jacob, *"What should your wages be?"* (**Genesis 29:15** NKJV)

Genesis 29:18 – *"Now Jacob loved Rachel; so he said, 'I will serve you seven years for Rachel your younger daughter.'"* NKJV

The plan was agreed upon, and Jacob worked seven years for the hand of Rachel in marriage. For Jacob, the seven years seemed like days due to his great love for Rachel.

When the time came for the marriage, Laban had a deceptive plan that would guarantee Jacob would continue on his payroll. A celebration feast was prepared, friends and family were gathered together, and Laban presented Jacob his new wife.

It was not until the morning after wedding night that the deception was discovered. With the morning light shining into the tent, Jacob saw he was sleeping with Leah, and he became angry.

How could this happen? Why did he not recognize it was Leah before morning? A couple things would help to understand. She was likely wearing a veil. There was no electricity in the tent. Jacob didn't check her ID. She entered his tent, and at that moment he wasn't concerned with any type of verification. All he knew was he was alone with the love of his life.

The obvious conclusion is that Leah was very much involved in both the plan and execution of this deception. She worked with her father in carrying out the process of deceiving Jacob. She willingly went through the process of preparing herself to look like a bride ready for wedding night. Laban presented her to Jacob as Rachel, and she said nothing. She entered Jacob's tent with him believing she was her beautiful sister, and she said nothing. Intimacy of wedding night was experienced, and she said nothing. Her personal identity and self-esteem was so low that in her search for value, she was willing to participate in this deception to gain a husband.

Jacob's reaction and his words of anger made the humiliation even worse.

Genesis 29:25 – *"What is this you have done to me? Was it not for Rachel that I served you? Why then have you deceived me?"* NKJV

Jacob felt betrayed and cheated. His seven years of devoted service were supposed to be rewarded with the compensation of Laban's beautiful daughter, Rachel. To Jacob, Leah was a breach of contract. He saw her as Laban trying to pass something off of less value than the agreed price. The agreement was Rachel the pretty one, not Leah.

Hurt and insult intensified for Leah with the agreement between Jacob and Laban concerning Rachel. Her younger sister would also become Jacob's wife.

Genesis 29:26-28 – *"Laban replied, 'It is not our custom here to give the younger daughter in marriage before the older one. Finish this daughter's bridal week; then we will give you the younger one also, in return for another seven years of work.' And Jacob did so. He finished the week with Leah, and then Laban gave him his daughter Rachel to be his wife."* NIV

Consider how all this made Leah feel. She gave herself to Jacob. She was viewed by her husband as a disappointment. Her husband didn't want her. Her husband wanted her younger sister. Can you imagine being married to someone who loves someone else? Can you imagine recognizing you are not your husband's first choice, and you represent a second string wife?

Leah had known Jacob for seven years. In those years she had grown in love with the young man. This love is evident due to her willingness to go along with the deception, and possibly secure Jacob as her husband. She so wanted the love to be mutual. Leah wanted Jacob to value her like she did him. Maybe after spending the night together the next morning he would look at her with the same love she had for him. This search for value in Jacob failed. He openly expressed how little he valued Leah.

Life was not good for Leah. Her husband felt deceived and tricked into marrying her. She allowed her father to use her. She gave herself to a man who did not love her. Her plan for a night of ecstasy that would begin a continuing, loving relationship failed. In her search for value she was nothing more than financial compensation for her father in a business deal. In her plan for romance to build into love she was a disappointment to a man feeling cheated. But she still believed she was *Made For More*.

******

I learned early in life that if there was going to be any encouragement in my personal life it was not coming from inside my home. Insulting words were flung daily. In my dad's anger and hatred for God, he went for the jugular. "You'll never amount to anything." "You were a mistake." Both were phrases used repeatedly.

As a teenager I found a personal value and an escape in weightlifting. I did not care for team sports. Having another adult male, like a coach, expressing disappointment in me by yelling at me was not appealing. Weightlifting was something I could do alone. I wasn't counting on anyone, and no one was counting on me. No team was involved. No coach was yelling. The only one I was competing against was myself. I loved it and found my personal escape in a plastic set of concrete filled weights and a steel bar.

As a teenage guy going to church with his mother my masculinity was under assault. Strength training and muscle building became my means of reinforcing being male. My goal was to get strong enough and muscled enough so no one would call me a sissy Christian.

Later in life I worked as a trainer, and was able to manage two health clubs. Weightlifting competition became an important part of my life for a number of years. My success was about average with a competition bench press of 325 pounds, squat of 480 pounds, and dead lift 460 pounds in a 181 body weight class. Not good enough for any records, but enough to have a few trophies drawing dust until I threw them away. Having muscles bulging and being stronger than anyone in the room was my search for value, but like Leah it soon faded and failed.

Years of pushing my body past pain levels, and forcing muscles and joints to take more stress than should be expected, resulted in a list of injuries. I've had 5 back surgeries with 3 spinal fusions, a total shoulder and hip replacement. Weightlifting and body building exercises gave great results until the body began to break down. I share with Leah the failure of the object of my search for value.

You may be like Leah too, searching for that source of personal value in life. This is a very legitimate search.

Don't let others define who you are.

Purpose and meaning are both something you desperately need. This search must take you outside yourself. It will not be found in personal accomplishments or achievements. This search will not end in a relationship with some special, good looking person. It must be found in something that lasts.

In a world of the temporary, fragile, inconsistent, and unreliable, discovering something that lasts has few options. I found this in my personal relationship with Jesus Christ. It is not about religion, it is all about relationship. Jesus became the relationship I longed for in a father. My young developmental years were filled with a longing for a relationship with an adult man I could trust and pattern my life after, but he never showed up. Eventually I was able to transfer the longing for that relationship to the one who was there all the time. Jesus became my mentor, my best friend, and the pattern I established as my personal target to follow with my life.

In Leah's life we see how ultimately more than just a relationship with a man became the target of her desire. She developed a desire for something more personal and lasting. She discovered there was something more fulfilling than seeking the affections of a man who didn't want to give them. She came to the realization of her need for an intimate relationship with God. It was that relationship that revealed to her the truth of being *Made For More*.

3. Rejected But Not Eliminated.

Leah, as a rejected woman, didn't look for excuses to quit. She looked for reasons to live. She didn't blame God. She didn't roll up in a ball and cry out for death. She didn't become angry and bitter. She didn't go into a deep depression. She didn't lose her ambition, hope, desire, or dreams for life. Instead she began having babies.

Leah bore Jacob six sons: Reuben, Simeon, Levi, Judah, Issachar, and Zebulun. Through Leah came six of the twelve tribes of Israel. With the birth of each son is recorded a word from Leah stating her expectations for her boys.

Leah chose the names for each of her six sons. Reuben was her first born and his name meant, "Behold, A Son!" With his birth Leah said: *"The Lord has surely looked on my affliction. Now therefore, my husband will love me."* NKJV **Genesis 29:32**

She proclaimed an expectation of Jacob's love. Her belief was that by giving him a son this would cause such a connection that he would give her the love she so craved, but he did not.

Simeon was her second son and his name meant, "Heard." In giving him this name she said, *"Because the Lord has heard that I am unloved, He has therefore given me this son also."* NKJV **Genesis 29:33**

Simeon's birth announcement revealed the topic of Leah's prayers, and how she was convinced God heard her. Her desperate cry from the broken heart of a woman unloved by her husband must have gained God's attention. Maybe now Jacob would love her, but he did not.

Leah named her third son Levi, and his name meant, "Attached." With his birth Leah said, *"Now this time my husband will become attached to me, because I have borne him three sons."* NKJV **Genesis 29:34**

Leah had now given Jacob three sons, while Rachel had given him none. Now the comparison changed from her being the one "without" to being the one "with". Surely there would be an attachment between her and the love of her life. There is no way a husband could not have a special bond of love and be completely attached to a wife who had given him three sons. She truly believed that this blessing would cause Jacob to love her, but it did not.

These years of comparison to Rachel brought an unhealthy competition between the two sisters. She may not be as pretty, but she could have babies while Rachel could not.

Genesis 30:1 — *"Now when Rachel saw that she bore Jacob no children, Rachel envied her sister, and said to Jacob. 'Give me children, or else I die!'"* NKJV

Competition became so extreme that Rachel declared she would rather die than let her sister win. Identity developed through comparison and competition will many times develop into pride. Pride speaking to Leah would say, "You're a better wife than your sister, you can give him babies." "Jacob will love you most because you are able to give him sons." Pride speaking to Rachel would say, "You've always been recognized as more attractive than your sister." "Who does she think she is threatening your position and trying to come between you and your husband?"

In the midst of all this turmoil, something happened in Leah's heart after the birth of Levi. Up to this time her heart's desire and life ambition was to gain Jacob's love. She had established Jacob as her life's desire. She was convinced that his love would bring her the joy and fulfillment she so craved. This had become so important, she was willing to enter a ruthless competition with her sister to win it.

These years of a competitive opponent relationship with her sister, finally brought a soul-searching recognition that Leah didn't like, and she was ready for change.

Where has your search for identity and purpose taken you? With so many images and all the varied information flooding your communication devices, your life is filled with options crying out to be your source of identity and purpose. It may be education, financial success, building a business, or being a media influencer. There is an endless supply of objectives crying out for your pursuit. Many feed a self-seeking craving for a popular well-known identity.

This pursuit may have even taken you to an unhealthy competition with some of the people closest to you. It is critical to hit the pause button and step back and ask yourself the important questions of: "Why is this important?" "Why am I pursuing this?" "Am I motivated by self-will and self-acclaim?"

"Who is getting the praise and recognition for my life pursuit?"

Reuben's birth gave the expectation of Jacob's love due to her giving him a son. Simeon's birth brought the recognition that God knew her heartbroken condition of being an unloved wife. Levi's birth gave the hope of an attachment being formed between her and Jacob.

A change came in Leah's heart with the birth of her fourth son. She experienced both a revelation of what was truly important and an establishing of a new pursuit in life. Now with this birth and the pronouncement of his name, there was no reference to her relationship with Jacob. It is at this time the focus of her life changes. No longer is her identity determined by her husband's love. No longer will she be defined by the comparison and competition with her sister. Now her focus goes to God.

Leah named her fourth son Judah. With his birth Leah proclaimed, *"Now I will praise the Lord."* **Genesis 29:35**

She went from seeking her identity and self-worth in her relationship with Jacob to finding her identity and value in her personal relationship with God. She quit seeking the approval of the one who didn't want to give it, to seeking the approval of the One who wanted to give it.

Leah chose to leave the constant comparison and competition with her sister to find there was more to life than the reflection in a mirror. She recognized there was more to life than being able to have babies. In God she found a source of an abundant and full life, and she was convinced He was worthy of her praise.

God can bring accomplishments, promotions, and achievements into your life that gives true value. Leah learned that once she established God as Lord of her life, that her relationship with Him brought true joy and fulfillment. He became the object of her life pursuit.

Her pathway to God was not a smooth one, but she made it. Now the strength of her identity in God brought praise. She knew who she was in God. The rejection would no longer define her. The competition with her sister was over. Her personal lacking was no longer an issue, she found her value elsewhere. You can clearly see how Leah was convinced that she was *Made For More*.

******

When I was 22 years old, dad walked up behind my mother while she was washing dishes, and began one of his rants. He was accusing her of having an affair with the pastor and declaring how church was a waste of time. She took her wet hands out of the dishwater, and turned around and laid both hands on him and shouted, "I rebuke you, Satan, in Jesus name!" At that moment dad started crying, and after a call to a Christian friend to come pray with him, he accepted Jesus as his Lord and Savior.

Dad was sincere about his salvation. His rebellion against God included cussing, drinking, and smoking cigarettes; so his dedication to God meant all that needed to go. The day after his salvation he gave Paula, my wife, two cartons of cigarettes. He told her, "I don't need them anymore!" And he never smoked another one. Paula took the cigarettes to the grocery store and traded them for baby formula. Jesus turned cigarettes into baby formula.

As hard as dad was against God he became tender and devoted to Him. He was an avid fisherman. He was a year-round, break-the-ice with-your-boat fisherman. He was one of those fishermen who dropped the annual cedar Christmas tree at the same spot in the lake each year to provide a spawning place for crappie. Then he made that spot his secret fishing hole only those in his boat knew about.

Once in his boat all his friends heard what Jesus had done for him, and they received an invitation to church. He felt if they were in his boat they couldn't get away, and he could possibly catch another one for Jesus.

Dad's salvation was real, and he lived it for the rest of his life until he died at 90 years old. For a number of years I got the pleasure of being his pastor.

Another major life event for me happened at 22 years old. The Lord opened the door for me to become a member of the Tulsa Fire Department. During my 17 years on the department there were so many experiences that helped shape my life. I worked on the fire company that had the first "jaws of life" in the City of Tulsa. This meant we worked every major car wreck in the city which placed our company in many life and death scenarios.

Attempting to help people in some of their worst life experiences is both heartbreaking and rewarding. It is so rewarding to know you are there for no other reason but to help. This gives such clarity of purpose and removes any distractions from that objective. Few things compare to saving someone's life or helping them through a life-devastating circumstance. It is heartbreaking in that not every victim is saved.

The schedule at the fire station allowed free time for me to study and finish my bachelor's degree. The duty shift schedule was on 24 hours and off 48 hours. This gave me the opportunity to also be a youth pastor for 13 years. I would work Saturday nights for a guy who raced stock cars, and he would work my Sunday mornings. It was a great trade off.

One of the most rewarding accomplishments while on the fire department happened on a day off. Our neighbor from next door ran into our house screaming for help, then turned and ran back home. I followed her to her backyard where a baby had just drowned in her swimming pool.

The baby's father was deaf and had watched a TV special about teaching babies to swim. Following the example he saw, he threw the baby into the water. The baby was able to make it back to him a couple of times. What he did not hear though was the baby gurgling, and her lungs filling with water. He threw her in again, and she went to the bottom. By the time I arrived the baby was lifeless, and her lips already had turned blue.

I will never forget the expression on that father's face. It was a combination of complete panic and terrible grief. When the father saw me he quickly handed me his baby. Without one word being spoken, it was obvious that he expected me to be able to do something to help. Having a lifeless baby handed over into my arms by a desperate father was a tremendous responsibility. It was critical that his trust placed in me brought a change to this terrible situation and gave his baby the help she desperately needed.

The fire department infant CPR training quickly kicked in. Within a short period of time the baby began breathing on her own. After being transported to the hospital and being examined for any side-effects, baby Amber was sent home completely healthy.

Today Amber is the mother of three children living a full and happy life. I received the Oklahoma State Firefighters Association Heroism Award for saving Amber's life, but there are heroes everywhere receiving no recognition. My personal definition of hero is being at the right place, at the right time, and willing to do the right thing. Thank God for preparing me for that afternoon. Thank God that He convinced me I was **Made For More**.

4. Thriving From Second

Leah gave birth to two more sons. Judah's birth brought her strong profession of faith when she declared, "Now I will praise the Lord." Years later she gave birth to Issachar and Zebulun. With Zebulun's birth she declared, *"God has endowed me with a good endowment; now my husband will dwell with me, because I have borne him six sons."* (**Genesis 30:20** NKJV

Now the insecurity was gone. She had a God-given endowment resulting in the assurance of a home and a lasting relationship with Jacob. She would not be kicked out like the child-bearing concubine, Hagar, was by Jacob's grandmother Sarah. She gave Jacob six sons and that would secure her place in the family. This was her endowment, her rightful position and identity in both the family of God and Jacob.

After 20 years of working for Laban, it was time for Jacob to head back home to Canaan. **Genesis 31:41** tells us Jacob worked for Laban 14 years for his two daughters, and 6 years for his herd of animals, and Laban changed his wages ten times. It had not been a great working relationship. Laban was consistent. He deceived Jacob, used Leah, and managed the affairs of his household all for his personal financial gain.

Now returning home, Jacob would also be reunited with Esau, his brother. They parted with a death threat from Esau. Much like Rachel and Leah, their relationship in the past had been one of competition. It was never a secret that Jacob was mom's favorite while Esau was favored by dad. Their family life had been dysfunctional, and there was a terrible conflict in the handling of both the birthright and the firstborn blessing.

Jacob didn't know how he would be received. So before coming face to face with his brother, he wanted to secure the safety of his family.

Genesis 33:2 – *"And he put the maidservants and their children in front, Leah and her children behind, and Rachel and Joseph last."* NKJV

In the event of an enemy attack, the furthest away from the front was the safest place. There they had the most protection. This positioning gave time for a counter-attack and provided the possibility that the enemy could be defeated before reaching them. It is obvious in this placing who Jacob wanted to be furthest from the enemy, and who he wanted in the place of greatest safety. It is a reminder to everyone who Jacob loved most. Joseph and Rachel would be placed the furthest away in this safest position. Without a question Joseph was the favorite son born to the love of his life, Rachel.

Over and over Jacob continues to reveal his special love for Rachel. Leah continues to be reminded that she is the second string wife. But with her heart change of, "Now I will praise the Lord", she is now willing to thrive from second.

The way you respond when you compete and lose reveals more about your character than when you win. When you win there are few options as a response. For the most part you are either gracious or arrogant. If gracious, you humbly acknowledge your opponent with words of encouragement, and attempt to downplay the victory. If arrogant, you flaunt the victory and belittle the loser as not being worthy of competing against you.

In losing, the response has a long list of options. There can be fault finding, blame, anger, frustration, regret, retaliation, quitting, accusations, and even humiliation with some level of depression. Losing brings a flood of emotions and the outcome can make you better or bitter.

Leah chose to be better. She didn't want to live with the label of an angry, bitter woman who lost the competition with her older sister.

Like Bartimaeus, she didn't want to be identified by limiting labels.

Mark 10:50 tells us Bartimaeus' response to Jesus calling out to him. *"And throwing aside his garment, he rose and came to Jesus."* NKJV *"Jewish Insights into the New Testament"* by Barbara Richmond helps to understand why Bartimaeus threw his garment from him. To be identified as a legitimate beggar, a license was given following an examination by someone in authority. The license was not a document, but a garment of a particular color and style. This garment was required to identify a beggar worthy of an offering.

When Bartimaeus, by faith, threw aside his garment, he was proclaiming his freedom from being labeled a beggar. He would no longer be Bartimaeus the blind beggar. Lying in the dirt alongside the road was not only a piece of cloth, but also a label identifying him with this tremendous life limitation.

Like Leah and Bartimaeus, do not allow your life to be restricted by labels. Yes, many labels are true and give a clear representation of the realities and details of your life. But just because it is the truth doesn't mean you have to accept it and continue living with it.

Leah would not live with the label "victim". She wanted her life to be identified by more than Rachel's ugly sister. She knew God had more for her life than being her dad's signing bonus for a new employee. She was more than an unloved, rejected wife. Each of these described the truth of her life, but she, like Bartimaeus, didn't want to wear them like a garment emphasizing her being worthy of pity.

***Do not allow your life to be
restricted by labels.***

******

I never had any intention nor even considered being in ministry. Standing in front of people and talking was never something easy for me.

My senior year English teacher knew I dreaded giving my oral book report so much that she let me come in after school and give it to her personally. I loved that lady!

My ministry experience started as a volunteer youth leader, then a part time youth pastor while also on the fire department. During this time my personal emphasis was working on my education and going through the process of ministry credentials. It was a busy time with a combination of marriage, raising two daughters, fire department, college, credentials, and part time youth ministry.

Life gets busy. In all the busyness of life it is critical to find your purpose. Life is more than an exhausting list of what you do, and how many accomplishments are accredited to your name. Why you do it stands as important as what you do.

Both the fire department and the youth ministry became my very fulfilling life purpose. Helping people in one of their most dramatic life-changing tragedies was so rewarding. Every time the alert tone sounded and the truck pulled out of the fire station was an opportunity to be the answer to someone's prayer for help. The opportunity to be an influence in the molding and shaping of a teenager's life is also so rewarding. At the time of working with them, there is little appreciation. But one of my life treasures now is to receive a message from one telling me about their accomplishments and the importance of those teenager years.

Chain of command on the Tulsa Fire Department was: rookie, private, relief-driver, driver, captain, chief. Personally, I believed driver was the best job, and that soon became my target. As driver you're responsible for transporting the fire company safely to the fire scene. Driving a firetruck with siren blaring and lights flashing the wrong way on a one-way street in downtown Tulsa is a rush. The captain is the boss and the driver is second in command.

As a youth pastor I was under the leadership of my senior pastor. Everything had to pass his approval. He was the one who gave guidelines and direction for accomplishing the God-given vision of the church. The pastor is the boss, and the youth pastor works under his mentorship and authority.

Leading from second doesn't carry with it the label of boss, incident commander, senior pastor, or most loved wife. You're not leading in the company, fire brigade, church, or the husband's affections for his wife. What you are leading is your personal life. You have both the responsibility and authority in the direction of your life.

Understanding this responsibility and authority is so important in leading your life. During every one of my parents-of-teenagers meetings held before an outing, I included this explanation. "If little Johnny goes with me on this outing, I accept complete responsibility for him, and you must give me total authority while he is in my care. If you tell me I'm completely responsible, but you don't want me to correct little Johnny and I have no authority over him, then he can't go".

I loved those teenagers, and together we took numerous missions trips, amusement park outings, camps, ski trips, canoe float trips, and an exhaustive list of other outings. There would be 50 to 100 teenagers entrusted to my care on each outing. My intent was to bring home the same number I took.

If little Johnny was doing something dumb that would either hurt him or someone else, I was going to exercise authority over him and get him back in line. This was never an option. This was a law. It was going to happen each and every time. The teenagers knew it and the parents knew it. Any gripe or complaint was met with "next time he can stay home".

It is frustrating to have responsibility without authority. If you have been given the responsibility for a given task, then you have every right to ask for and expect the authority for the process to accomplish it. It is micro-managing to give someone an assignment and then dictate every step in how to accomplish it.

You have both responsibility and authority for your life. As a teenager, parents or guardians can't oversee your behavior 24 hours a day. You'll be out of sight, out of range, out of hearing distance. From a young age you learn how to get gone, get lost, and get away. Your true character is revealed by what you do when no one is watching.

Marriage places an emphasis on responsibility and authority. Sharing marriage vows and entering into the life commitment of love comes with tremendous responsibilities.

Ephesians 5:29 explains how the love of the husband for his wife comes with the responsibility of nourishing and cherishing her. Nourishing indicates he is responsible for helping her to be the best she can be. Cherishing establishes the husband as the one responsible for her self-esteem. Cherishing communicates how special she is with both words and actions. Cherishing is the husband convincing her that he believes she is the prettiest woman on the planet. If the wife feels unattractive with a low self-esteem and fragile self-image, then the husband is not fulfilling his responsibility. This was Jacob's responsibility he did not fulfill for Leah.

Ephesians 5:33 tells us the responsibility of the wife is found in her respect for her husband. One of the greatest ways of showing disrespect to a man is to communicate whatever he does it is never enough. The husband's self-esteem of being a good husband, a good father, a good provider, a good protector, a good lover is determined by the wife. If the husband feels like a loser with a low self-esteem and fragile self-image, then the wife is not fulfilling her responsibility.

In marriage both husband and wife must accept their responsibility for each other. With this responsibility they have the authority to make the decisions which are necessary in bringing the needed change. Authority must be taken over your words and actions in how you treat your spouse.

You have both the responsibility and authority in the direction of your life.

You get to make your own choices. You determine your character. You choose if you'll live according to Biblical principles pleasing to God, or not. You have that God-given authority. But you are also responsible. You must take responsibility for your personal life and actions. It is not your momma's fault. It is not your daddy's fault. It is not your grandparent's fault. It is no one else's fault. No one else is responsible. You must own it.

Leah owned her attitude in thriving from second without anger, hate, nor bitterness; because she knew she was ***Made For More***.

5. From Second To First

Leah's perseverance over the years of being a second string wife gave her the qualifications necessary for her next role in the household of Jacob. Leah's refusal to build her self-esteem by standing on the back of someone crushed by her evaluation, set her up for a promotion. Her attitude of praising and worshiping God in the midst of all the negative circumstances was about to be rewarded.

Genesis 35:19 – *"So Rachel died and was buried on the way to Ephrath (that is Bethlehem).*NKJV

Rachel's death placed Leah in the position of number one wife. Her beautiful sister was no longer competing for Jacob's love. Leah was given what she craved for years. She had the attention of Jacob without the distraction of her sister.

Jacob lived another 30 years after the death of Rachel. We can trace this timeline using the information given concerning Rachel's first born son Joseph.

Genesis 37:2 – Joseph was 17 years old.
Genesis 41:36 – Joseph was 30 years old.
Genesis 47:28 – Jacob lived in Egypt 17 years.

At the time of Rachel's death Joseph was approximately 17 years old. From 17 to 30, Joseph had been a slave and in prison for 13 years. Then with the God-given favor of being second in command in Egypt, Joseph brought his family into Egypt. Jacob lived 17 years in Egypt which is a total of 30 years since Rachel's death. We are not given the time of Leah's death, but her time as Jacob's number one wife could be as long as 30 years.

What would her heart be for Jacob now as his wife? Would her years of losing the competition with her sister now become a wall of bitterness between them? Would she have some vendetta against Jacob in an attempt to get even for years of neglect? Leah could easily have developed a disdain for Jacob. From the insult of wedding night to the years of being reminded she was not the love of his life, could have built in Leah a "get even" heart of hatred for Jacob.

Leah winning the baby-having competition could have developed arrogance and pride in her heart towards Jacob. She did give him 6 sons. She was responsible for half of the 12 tribes of Israel. No one could touch her record. Jacob would not be enjoying a large, productive family if it were not for Leah. Pride and arrogance could have developed in Leah's heart causing her to believe that Jacob owed her sincere devotion and unwavering respect as the mother of his children.

We have no details recorded in scripture concerning the relationship between Jacob and Leah during these years. But we do have information concerning a decision Jacob made which indicates how special this relationship became. All of these possibilities of what could have happened in Leah's heart didn't. In this one decision, Jacob revealed how Leah became the wife God wanted her to be. She so conducted her life that Jacob couldn't do anything but respond with love.

Before his death Jacob requested to be taken back to the land of Israel and be buried with his fathers. When he secured this promise from Joseph and his other sons, Jacob gave specific details about the location of his burial.

Genesis 49:31 – *"There they buried Abraham and Sarah his wife, there they buried Isaac and Rebekah his wife, and there I buried Leah."* NKJV

Leah made it! She became the love of Jacob's life.

Here in this request concerning his burial, Jacob compared his love for Leah with that between Abraham and Sarah, Isaac and Rebekah. Just as important as establishing the location of his final resting place was also the finalizing who would be at his side. It was not

"Here Lies Jacob And Rachel." It was "Here Lies Jacob And Leah."

No details are given in scripture, but the evidence near the end of his life indicates that for Jacob, Leah thrived as first wife. Jacob's love growing for her reveals Leah's heart desire was simply to be the wife God wanted her to be.

******

God's will and plan for your life does not have to be complicated. You just have to start moving. Just as the wind cannot move a ship that has an anchor set deep in the ocean floor, fear and the feeling of inadequacy make you immovable for God's leading. You must raise the anchor for God to direct your life towards His will. If you wait until you are completely qualified and totally prepared you'll never move. Everyone who finishes well had a starting line.

Ecclesiastes 11:4 – *"He who observes the wind will not sow, and he who regards the clouds will not reap."* NKJV

This one verse teaches how you can become completely shut down from achieving your dreams. Here we see an illustration of how you can over evaluate the challenges you face to the point that they become obstacles paralyzing your forward progress.

In farming, the goal is to get the seed into the ground and with time that seed becomes produce. Once ripe for harvest the produce is reaped and gathered into the barn. Wind has a negative effect on seed. Seed that is thrown and caught by the wind veers off course and is unproductive. If you're looking for a reason to not sow then observe the wind.

Ripe produce has a brief time span from being ready to harvest and being rotten in the field. Rain rots produce setting in a field. There is nothing of value to gather when the crop is covered by mud from a soaking rain. If you want a reason for not reaping, then look for any indication of a cloud that could possibly produce rain.

Excuses sought out will be found. If you make yourself sensitive to the feeling of wind there will always be enough to delay the sowing. Even the smallest cloud can cause your mind to anticipate rain if that is what you're looking for. Ideal conditions are rare. If you wait until you're smart enough, talented enough, gifted enough, prepared enough; you'll never move.

God's will is not determined by perfect conditions. Sometimes you have to sow even with the wind blowing. There are times you'll be forced to reap even on a cloudy day. You must be willing to move even when conditions are not ideal. Roadblocks are not always there to halt your forward advance. Sometimes they redirect, and sometimes they are obstacles you overcome that make you stronger. God uses both, and it is critical to seek Him during a life roadblock so He can reveal to you if it is to redirect or overcome.

The path of least resistance is not necessarily the right one. Faith is stepping out without all the answers. Faith is stepping out without all the resources. Faith is stepping out without knowing what the outcome will be. You'll never enjoy the fullness of life where faith wants to take you unless you take that first step.

Ecclesiastes 11:6 – *"In the morning sow your seed, and in the evening do not withhold your hand; for you do not know which will prosper. Either this or that, or whether both alike will be good."* NKJV

Productivity and success are not determined by ease of work, but neither will be achieved if you don't move. You must believe that God will help you overcome the obstacles. It is not your grit, your determination, your dedication, or your personal ability that gains the victory. It is the hand of God. God can calm the wind or use the wind to guide the seed to the most fertile soil. God can remove the clouds, or leave them for shade as the reapers work in the heat of the day. Wind and clouds should not stall forward progress, but if you look for an excuse you will find it.

In most every achievement there are excuses for why it should have never begun. With God on your side the source of excuses like wind and clouds can become assets for success.

At my high school graduation if I had been asked the details of my future, it would not be what I have lived. I didn't have a clue concerning the direction of my life. No one in my family had a college degree. No one in my family had been in ministry. No one had been a professional firefighter. No one had been in the health club business. I had no examples before me. I had no one to counsel me of where and how God would direct my life.

In my self-evaluation I was willing to admit to myself, "You don't know anything." Rather than trying to slide through or fake it, I found it liberating to accept the honesty of that revelation. Soon I also realized, "You won't accomplish anything of value by accident." These two revelations became the motivation for me to raise my anchor and begin to move.

You must not expect success or achievement to be given to you. Once you take possession of your God-given goals and dreams it's time to set the alarm and get ready to work for them. There is a saying by famous motivational speaker, Zig Zigler, that I love. It is, "The person who aims at nothing will hit it every time." A target is critical in both beginning to move and knowing in which direction to move.

Even in your relationship with God you must establish goals. You won't accidentally read through your Bible in a year. You'll have to read approximately 4 chapters every day. You won't accidently find time every day to pray. You may have to set your alarm, or turn off the TV.

God's will and plan for your life does not have to be complicated. You just have to start moving.

God has a divine purpose for you. No one on the planet will come in contact with the exact people you will. There is nothing more important to God than people. Success, achievement, productivity are not found in building a bank account. Prosperity in God's kingdom is not found in something as trivial as money and possession. It is found in the number of lives that have been changed for good due to your influence.

Your life has God's fingerprints all over it. The beginning of your life was orchestrated and ordered by the sovereignty of God. You were born when God wanted. You were fashioned according to God's design. You were born into the family of God's plan. You have a purpose that can only be found in your life obedience to God.

John 10:27 – *"My sheep hear My voice, and I know them, and they follow Me."* NKJV

Hearing the voice of Jesus is more than at the beginning of a relationship with Him. It starts at the beginning but continues as you change your life's cravings and desires to live in His will. Leah's motives and intent changed with Judah's birth, and she began to praise God. In like manner, change comes into your life as you develop a relationship of trust and follow the voice of Jesus.

Noise from your own heart is trying to silence the voice of Jesus. The volume of your personal mind-set can be so loud that any leading and guiding from Jesus is met with a cynical unbelief. Your pre-determined answer can be so established that the anchor is set, and you refuse to listen to any other options. Your specific goals and life dreams can so consume your ambition that you pressure God to lead and guide only towards their fulfilment.

Leah had this noise trying to drown out God's voice. Her mind-set was to push aside her sister and become Jacob's wife. Her pre-determined answer was that by having babies Jacob would love her. For her, the dream of being in a marriage relationship of mutual love with Jacob became her identity, and she expected God to lead only towards the fulfillment of that dream.

Like Leah, you must overcome life obstacles and keep them from parlaying your forward progress. Leah refused to allow rejection, insults, labels, and belittling to define her. She was more than the ugly sister and she knew it.

Through her experiences, Leah was eventually able to recognize the difference between noise and God's voice. If God was worthy of her praise then He should be given the rightful position as Lord of her life. Praise and worship is hypocrisy if Jesus is not Lord of your life.

Leah had a God-given purpose, and she was willing to pull up the anchor, ignore the wind, and use the clouds for shade; as she moved forward following the voice of God.

6. Enduring Legacy

It is amazing to see the many lives influenced by Leah. Our world would not be what it is today without Leah. She has often been referred to as the "ugly sister." This insult in her identity did not hold Leah back. God reveals through her the potential that is found in you. The story of this woman who is responsible for so much began with a personal insult in her appearance. Beyond any question or doubt, Leah was convinced she was **Made For More**.

From Leah came Levi. From Levi came the priesthood along with Moses and Aaron. Moses wrote the first 5 books of the Bible. Through Moses came the 10 commandments and specifications in worshipping God. Moses was also responsible for leading God's people out of Egyptian bondage. Ezra was a priest of the tribe of Levi and wrote the book in the Bible bearing his name.

Without Leah our Bible would not have Genesis, Exodus, Leviticus, Numbers, Deuteronomy, or Ezra. Without Leah, Moses would not have been available to be used by God in his many accomplishments.

From Leah came Judah. From Judah came Boaz, Jessie, David, and Solomon. David wrote many of the Psalms. Solomon wrote Proverbs, Ecclesiastes, and the Song Of Solomon. That is 10 books of the Bible that can be traced back to the linage of Leah.

Without Leah there would be no David to receive the promise that through his lineage would be born the Messiah. David was in the genealogy of Jesus Christ. So if there was no David there would be no Jesus. Without Jesus there would be no savior, no salvation, no forgiveness, no hope, and no eternal life.

God chose to do it this way. From His divine perspective and His complete sovereignty, He made the decision that this one woman would hold the key to the future of all humanity.

1 Peter 1:20 teaches us that even before the world was created, Jesus was established to be God's sacrifice for sin. Jesus would be the Lamb of God to be killed and provide redemption for all mankind. None of the process was a surprise to God. He knew and even planned for Leah to be in this process.

Not bad for the "ugly sister." What a legacy for the one everyone overlooked. Her dad used her as part of a deceptive scheme in a business deal. Her husband openly proclaimed his disappointment in her after their wedding night. Her years of being the second wife gave her constant reminders of her husband's true love. But through it all in the depth of her heart she was convinced that she was *Made For More*.

******

70

How about you? What is the challenge you're dealing with? Has the influence around you tried to convince you of how inadequate you are? When you look in the mirror do you see an ugly sister, a confused teenager, a damaged young adult, a neglected wife, a man lacking integrity and character? It may be time to develop spiritual backbone and persevering grit.

God never said it would be easy. What He did say is that you'd never be alone.

There are a variety of different positions held concerning God's will. Some say God is too busy to be involved in your personal life, and you should not bother Him for help in working out the details. Others attempt to persuade that in God's sovereignty your life will result in His will regardless of your personal choices. Another is that God's will gives a life free from problems and difficulty, and that hard times surface only when you step out of God's will. I don't agree with any of these.

I believe God's will is God's best for your life. He will be involved in every aspect you invite Him. He is the source of every good thing that comes into your life. He will be your strength in the hard times, and through them He will build character and integrity. Living your life in God's will is the best life to live.

Believing that quality of life is based upon the ease of life is wrong. It is deceiving to be convinced that things coming easy, with little to no effort, are best. It is wrong to believe that life becomes worse as difficulty increases. In this thinking God's best is always easy, and difficult means you are out of God's will. In this thinking if things become difficult then you must turn around and go the other way to be in God's will. These thoughts are so misleading.

God's best is not always easy. Difficult doesn't mean you are out of God's will. There are times that if you turn and move away from difficulty you will miss God!

Romans 5:3,4 – *"... we also glory in tribulations, knowing that tribulation produces perseverance; and perseverance, character; and character hope."* NKJV

Strong character traits are developed through the difficult. An abusive father using her for financial gain was a terrible part of Leah's past. Stuck in a marriage relationship with a man who didn't love her was a time she endured. Leah getting caught up in a competition of having babies and giving birth to six boys and one girl was not like visiting a spa or being on vacation. She was one tough girl!

Leah built her strength through enduring the difficult. Her life reveals to us how God wants to provide for us far more than just a superficial standard of living. Living in God's will is living life to the fullest. Leah experienced God's blessing of growing old with Jacob. She ultimately received the compassionate love of the one she fell in love with as a young lady. Leah lived her dream.

Life to the fullest is not being dominated by emptiness and disappointment. It is rising above the mediocrity and mundane and living with expectation. It is living free from guilt, condemnation, and regret. It is knowing God has a plan and a purpose for your life and He can shine through every circumstance both easy and difficult.

John 15:11 – *"I have told you this so that My joy may be in you and that your joy may be complete."* NIV

There is a joy God has for you living in His will. God can be trusted. To reach this target you must face your challenges with the assurance that through God you can accomplish great things. You will have to silence the noise coming from within attempting to convince of your inadequacy. Your future is great in God, and He desperately wants to convince you that you were **Made For More.**

Leah's Story

[Selected excerpts are taken from the New Living Translation]

Gen 29:14...After Jacob had been there about a month, 15 Laban said to him, "You shouldn't work for me without pay just because we are relatives. How much do you want?"

16 Now Laban had two daughters: Leah, who was the oldest, and her younger sister, Rachel. 17 Leah had pretty eyes, but Rachel was beautiful in every way, with a lovely face and shapely figure. 18 Since Jacob was in love with Rachel, he told her father, "I'll work for you seven years if you'll give me Rachel, your younger daughter, as my wife."

19 "Agreed!" Laban replied. "I'd rather give her to you than to someone outside the family."

20 So Jacob spent the next seven years working to pay for Rachel. But his love for her was so strong that it seemed to him but a few days. 21 Finally, the time came for him to marry her. "I have fulfilled my contract," Jacob said to Laban. "Now give me my wife so we can be married."

22 So Laban invited everyone in the neighborhood to celebrate with Jacob at a wedding feast. 23 That night, when it was dark, Laban took Leah to Jacob, and he slept with her. 24 And Laban gave Leah a servant, Zilpah, to be her maid.

25 But when Jacob woke up in the morning — it was Leah! "What sort of trick is this?" Jacob raged at Laban. "I worked seven years for Rachel. What do you mean by this trickery?"

26 "It's not our custom to marry off a younger daughter ahead of the firstborn," Laban replied. 27 "Wait until the bridal week is over, and you can have Rachel, too — that is, if you promise to work another seven years for me." 28 So Jacob agreed to work seven more years. A week after Jacob had married Leah, Laban gave him Rachel, too. 29 And Laban gave Rachel a servant, Bilhah, to be her maid. 30 So Jacob slept with Rachel, too, and he loved her more than Leah. He then stayed and worked the additional seven years.

31 But because Leah was unloved, the LORD let her have a child, while Rachel was childless.

[Jacob's Sons]

Genesis 35: *These are the names of the twelve sons of Jacob:*

23 The sons of Leah were Reuben (Jacob's oldest son), Simeon, Levi, Judah, Issachar, and Zebulun.

24 The sons of Rachel were Joseph and Benjamin.

25 The sons of Bilhah, Rachel's servant, were Dan and Naphtali.

26 The sons of Zilpah, Leah's servant, were Gad and Asher.

[Death of Rachel]

Genesis 35:16 *Leaving Bethel, they traveled on toward Ephrath (that is, Bethlehem). But Rachel's pains of childbirth began while they were still some distance away. 17 After a very hard delivery, the midwife finally exclaimed, "Don't be afraid — you have another son!" 18 Rachel was about to die, but with her last breath she named him Ben-oni; the baby's father, however, called him Benjamin. 19 So Rachel died and was buried on the way to Ephrath (that is, Bethlehem). 20 Jacob set up a* *stone monument over her grave, and it can be seen there to this day.*

[Death of Leah]

Genesis 49:29 *Then Jacob told them, "Soon I will die. Bury me with my father and grandfather in the cave in Ephron's field. 30 This is the cave in the field of Machpelah, near Mamre in Canaan, which Abraham bought from Ephron the Hittite for a permanent burial place. 31 There Abraham and his wife Sarah are buried. There Isaac and his wife, Rebekah, are buried. And there I buried Leah. 32 It is the cave that my grandfather Abraham bought from the Hittites." 33 Then when Jacob had finished this charge to his sons, he lay back in the bed, breathed his last, and died.*

NLT

End Notes:

Holy Bible Versions as follows:

NIV - New International Version

NKJV – New King James Version

NLT – New Living Translation

Page 49 Richmond, Barbara *"Jewish Insights into the New Testament"*. Thunderbird Press, FL 1996

Made in the USA
Monee, IL
24 October 2024

a1ff6e67-a6b9-4fdf-854e-048f8ad1f7d2R01